This book is dedicated to all those who have

stared up at the stars and dared to question,

and to those who believe that *science* and *faith*

can point the way forward.

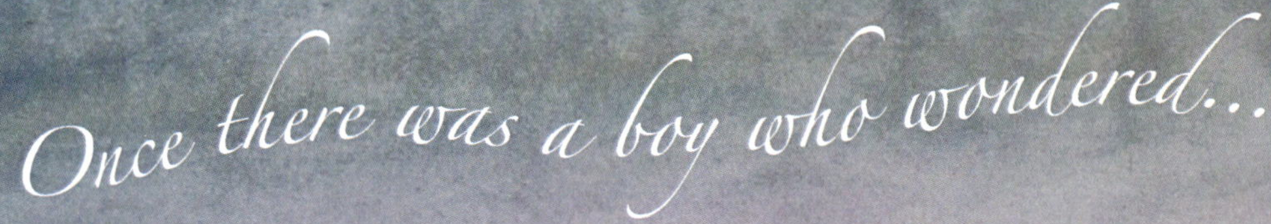

Quintessential Stories
146 Spirit Ridge Lane
Camano Island, WA 98282
quintessentialstories.com
quintestories@gmail.com

Library of Congress Control Number : 2024909825
Library of Congress Cataloging-in-Publication Data
Names: Asplund, Kurt Cameron, 1953- author. |
Adebayo, Kathryn Grace, 1992- illustrator.
Title: Who Is God? / By Kurt Asplund ; Illustrated by Kathryn Adebayo.
Description: First edition. | Camano Island, WA: Quintessential Stories
[40] p. : col. ill ; cm.
ISBN 979-8-9903002-0-0 (softcover) | 979-8-9903002-1-7 (hardcover)
Subjects: God (from perspective of science and faith) ›
Children's Literature › Science, Nature & How It Works ›
Mystery & Wonders › Religion & Spirituality › Who Is God?

Printed in the United States of America
10 9 8 7 6 5 4
First Edition

Book and Cover Design
by Kathryn Adebayo
The art for this book was created
with watercolors and acrylics
and edited digitally.

"Huge thanks to my dear wife, Leslie,
whose editorial contributions were invaluable
and whose loving support will never be forgotten." – K. Asplund

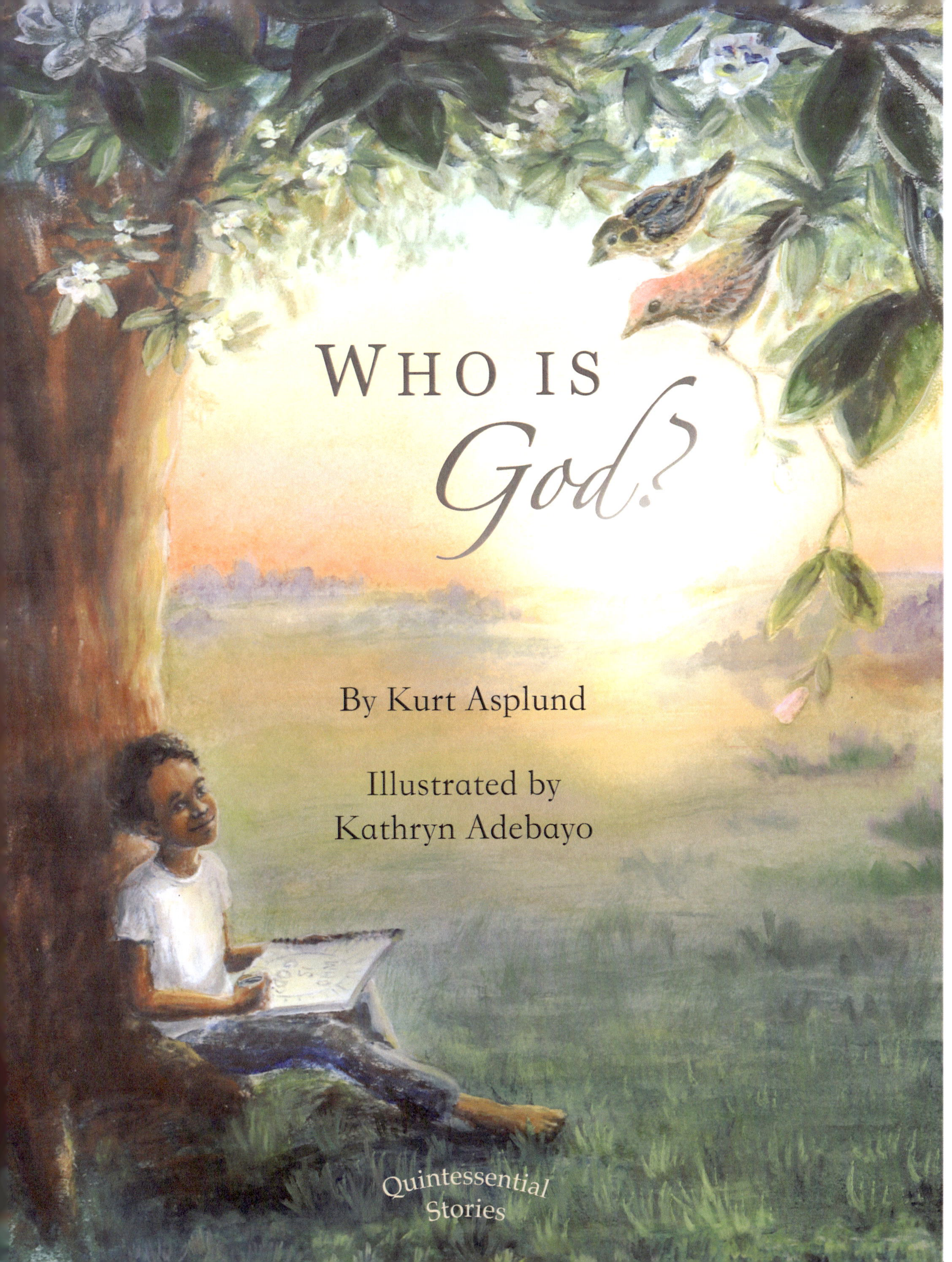

WHO IS
God?

By Kurt Asplund

Illustrated by
Kathryn Adebayo

Quintessential
Stories

If it were not for the Sun,
all the things that we see
around us – the birds, the
trees, the flowers, the
animals, our families,
ourselves – would not exist.

Like a giant rock,

the Earth would just drift

in the cold and darkness of space.

The Sun provides light
and life to the world.

God is like that.

When the clouds cover the Sun,
the Sun does not go away.

When our place on the Earth spins away
from the Sun, then nighttime comes.
It may seem like the Sun left us…

…but, actually, it is shining as brightly
as ever on the other side of the Earth.

The Sun does not go away.
We turn away.

It's nice to know that, even in the
darkest night, the Sun is still shining.

God is like that.

Suppose the light
shining down from
God is actually Love.

Then, like the rays of the Sun,
this Love would never go away.

But it's hard to believe we're
surrounded by love when bad things
happen that we don't understand…

…when it truly seems that all is lost,

and the Sun is just a
distant memory.

Sometimes it's hard to remember
that Love has the power
to mend a broken heart.

Create in me a pure
heart, O my God....
and by the light of
Thy Glory, reveal
unto me Thy path.

There are so many questions!
Why are we here on planet Earth?
Where does the Sun come from?
Why is there so much pain and
suffering?

Scientists can tell us a lot about our world,
but they admit that there are some things
that will remain a mystery.

God is like that.

Scientists suggest that the universe started
about 14 billion years ago!

First there was nothing.

Then there was a universe with millions of
galaxies, each galaxy with billions of stars
like our very own star, the Sun. If God
didn't do that, then who did?

Whoever did it must be very
great and very powerful!

Some say it was God, some say it was Allah,
and others say the Great Spirit or Yahweh.

But the most important thing is how we hold
the light of this Great Being in our hearts.

When we're
filled with this light,
we see things differently,
and answers appear as if
out of nowhere.

When we share this light with others,
then love comes streaming back to us

from our family,

our friends,
our teachers…

even from our
beloved pet!

It's hard to describe love, but
we can feel it when it's there,
and we know it exists.

Love is the very reason we
are all here on planet Earth.

Imagine a Being greater than the Sun –
a Being that radiates Love so strongly
that we can feel it in our hearts,
even on a cloudy day.

God is like that!

Kurt Asplund, MA – a naturalist, playwright, and mental health counselor – wrote the first draft of *Who Is God?* in one sitting, as he gazed out over the forest, bay, and inlets below his house on beautiful Camano Island in the Pacific Northwest.

Kathryn (Katy) Adebayo has always loved art that portrays the noble and reverent qualities of the human spirit. She hopes that the reader catches a glimpse of that spirit in the paintings of the boy in this story.

*

Both Kurt and Katy draw their inspiration from the Bahá'í Writings and from the sacred scriptures of the world's great religions. They wish to acknowledge that the Sun metaphor in this story, which is used to describe the power of God's eternal light, can hardly do justice to the glory and majesty of the One Who created the universe.

The quote on page 21 is an excerpt of a prayer by Bahá'u'lláh.

"How can I claim to
have known Thee, when the
entire creation is bewildered by
Thy mystery, and how can I confess
not to have known Thee, when, lo,
the whole universe proclaimeth
Thy Presence and testifieth
to Thy truth?"

Bahá'u'lláh